NATIONAL BUS COMPANY SERVICE VEHICLES

VEHICLES

1972–1986: ANOTHER LOOK

Michael Hitchen

AMBERLEY

First published 2023

Amberley Publishing
The Hill, Stroud
Gloucestershire, GL5 4EP

www.amberley-books.com

Copyright © Michael Hitchen, 2023

The right of Michael Hitchen to be identified
as the Author of this work has been asserted
in accordance with the Copyright, Designs and
Patents Act 1988.

ISBN 978 1 3981 1503 3 (print)
ISBN 978 1 3981 1504 0 (ebook)

British Library Cataloguing in Publication Data.
A catalogue record for this book is available from
the British Library.

Origination by Amberley Publishing.
Printed in the UK.

Introduction

Continuing on from my first book on NBC service vehicles, which was published by Amberley in 2018, here is another selection of photographs to compliment the first volume. Reference between the two books is helpful as some vehicles referred to here can be found in the first book. The erstwhile National Bus Company was the largest bus company in the world and like any large organisation, it required auxiliary vehicles to support its core activities of transporting the public in England and Wales. When the corporate image was introduced in 1972, variety was the norm; fleet makeups were very different between each company. Formed of around thirty-six local constituent companies and the 'NATIONAL' Central Activities Group to operate long distance and tour coaches, every company had its own service vehicle fleet to support its operations, varying from heavy vehicle recovery to driver training and every other facet to keep the fleet operational. Well photographed and documented were the former PSV conversions, driver trainers, tree loppers or towing buses. Being based on a bus attracted the photographers' lens, but the commercial vehicles owned by the NBC, in an era when film was precious, were often overlooked by enthusiasts at the time. The vehicles used were typical of the period: virtually all of British manufacture, Ford, BMC or Leyland, the same as seen in everyday use on the roads. Usually painted in the same livery as the bus fleet, each fleet had a selection of small and medium sized vans, LDs, J4s, JU250, Sherpas, Escorts, Transits, and a number of larger open lorries, usually Bedford TK/TLs or Ford 'D's, some of which would be fitted with hydraulic cranes. Apart from the commercial vehicles, fleets could also contain oddments such as Land Rovers, fuel tankers, platform lifts, road sweepers, small cranes, tractors and forklifts. Occasionally even a motorbike, as Southern Vectis had. Certain fleets also operated tractor units with articulated trailers, either for driver training, or to move fuel tankers. Bristol, Hants & Dorset and Crosville all had tractor units. Every NBC constituent fleet operated at least one heavy recovery vehicle, which would usually have the bodywork rebuilt by the company often using bus body parts. The AEC Matador chassis prevailed, and the finished vehicles were often stylish and therefore fortunately were well photographed. After the Matador the AEC Mandator was a popular choice as a replacement, though these vehicles retained their Ergomatic cab often with International Wreckers equipment. The next most popular lorries used for recovery was the Ford D, a common type on the roads of Britain at the time. A few of the ex-Army Canadian Fords lasted into the corporate era with Bristol, Southdown, United and Western National (Royal Blue). Sadly none lasted long enough to receive full corporate livery. Albion, Bedford and Foden also featured as heavy recovery vehicles but only in small numbers.

Though the National Bus Company was a state-owned organisation, each constituent managed its service fleet independently. Where a company owned only one heavy recovery vehicle, it would be supplemented by converted buses, for towing duties from larger garages; some companies such as United had a mix of lorries and former bus recoveries. Western National was unusual in only using heavy recovery lorries for its dedicated recovery needs, and United Counties was similar in preferring to use lorries, though it did have one converted bus in use in 1972. Crosville in the early 1970s purchased a number of Land Rovers to cover much of its routine towing needs, until regulations changed and they were no longer suitable. Small companies such as Cumberland, Southern Vectis and Provincial could manage with a single recovery vehicle for much of the time.

Though initially directed by NBC headquarters to paint service vehicles in white with large 'NATIONAL' lettering similar to the NBC coaches, fleets mainly chose their own liveries, usually the same as there buses, but others such as Hants & Dorset chose to paint many of their commercial vehicles yellow or white, while East Midland/Mansfield were almost anonymous. West Yorkshire used a non-standard dark green for many years, while Southern Vectis adopted a half green/half white similar to the dual-purpose buses of the era, and like Red & White retained the pre-corporate gold underlined lettering on some of its service fleet.

The reader will appreciate that information concerning most of these vehicles is scarce, therefore I have recorded dates of conversion/purchase to the best of my knowledge, and the listed allocations would change over time; finding what vehicles were in a service fleet was rarely available and was often dependent on the company. I have included a selection of service vehicle lists from official sources, to give the reader some idea of an operator's fleet, but in many cases the information was not available. Crosville and Trent published professionally printed and illustrated fleet lists complete with all the service fleet. Other companies such as Hants & Dorset, Provincial and Southern Vectis produced simple copied fleet lists, but included service vehicles. London

Country details were readily available, published by LOTS, Capital Transport and Ian Allan; Southdown and Maidstone & District/East Kent were available through their enthusiast clubs fleet lists. PSV circle histories occasionally included service vehicles; Crosville, Eastern Counties, Eastern National, Hants & Dorset and Western National being example that do, though these only covered the period up to the last time they were updated. Enthusiast seeking more details of United Counties should refer to Roger M. Warwick's

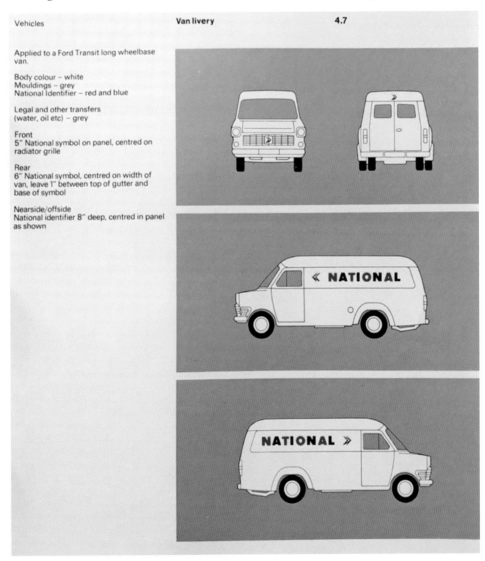

Vehicles	Van livery	4.7

Applied to a Ford Transit long wheelbase van.

Body colour – white
Mouldings – grey
National Identifier – red and blue

Legal and other transfers
(water, oil etc) – grey

Front
5" National symbol on panel, centred on radiator grille

Rear
6" National symbol, centred on width of van, leave 1" between top of gutter and base of symbol

Nearside/offside
National identifier 8" deep, centred in panel as shown

NBC Corporate Manual 4.7 Vehicles Van Livery

When the National Bus company issued its design manual for the new corporate image in 1972 only one page was allocated for guidance on painting service vehicles; a few companies followed this directive, usually only for a short time, Trent being a good example, but the majority applied their own diverse interpretations to their auxiliary vehicle liveries.

An Illustrated History of United Counties Omnibus Company Limited, which he published in several parts, each covering different eras, and included full details and lists of service vehicles the company used at time and some photos of vehicles. Occasionally details can be obtained from like-minded enthusiasts who fortunately recorded details at the time. These can appear on social media sites.

Photographs in this volume are new, although a couple of these vehicles have appeared in the first volume but have been included for a different view or interest point. Thanks go to Dave Mant, Glen Bubb, Mike Street and Lindsey Young for their kind assistance with photos and to John Harrington, who has done much invaluable research, especially concerning AEC Matador conversions, on the subject of service vehicles for many years.

Today's bus scene is very different. Recovery is undertaken through contracts. Vans can still be found, even carrying the companies livery, though dedicated driver training vehicles often appear like PSV vehicles. The National Bus Company disappeared from our roads in 1986, and with it the unified organisation across England and Wales. Fortunately interest in service vehicles and this aspect of operations is better served than ever via social media and photo sharing websites. I hope the reader enjoys a further look at this unusual and obscure subject, which fortunately in the subsequent years has grown in interest thanks to the internet, which will hopefully save very rare and possibly unique photographs for future generations.

Alder Valley 1050, t/p 473 RD

Thames Valley purchased a former Military AEC Matador in 1960 and rebuilt it at its Reading workshop with a stylish body and newer style AEC grill. Originally numbered ED1, it became number 15 with the formation of Alder Valley, who painted it NBC poppy red. It is seen here recovering an unidentified Leyland National that had received substantial damage. It had been repainted yellow and received the number 1050.

Alder Valley 1052, t/p 141 AA, Aldershot Bus Station

Aldershot & District bought two government surplus AEC Matadors in the 1960s. Both retained much of their original cab and bodywork. 1052 was originally numbered 32 becoming number 1 with the formation of Alder Valley and being allocated to Aldershot garage, which was painted on the cab door. The company later painted all its recovery lorries yellow, as seen here.

Alder Valley 2, t/p 590 AA, National Welsh Central Workshops, Bulwark, Chepstow

Aldershot & Districts second Matador was allocated to Guildford garage. Converted in 1965 and numbered 42, the two were near identical. Numbered 2 by Alder Valley, it would be renumbered 1053 in June 1978. Seen a long way from its home garage, two stands outside the National Welsh Central Workshops in Bulwark, Chepstow, probably recovering a broken-down coach.

Alder Valley 1105, 413 COR, Reading Garage, June 1980

Dennis Loline driver trainer 1105 (413 COR) stands withdrawn in the yard of Reading garage. The company used both Lolines and Bristol Lodekkas for training duties, reflecting the joint origins of the company. Converted from bus 413, and previously number 13 in the Alder Valley service fleet, it had retaining poppy red livery before renumbering and gaining yellow livery. Unfortunately, this vehicle was destroyed by fire on this spot soon after.

Alder Valley 46 (GGM 63W), Reading Bus Station

Alder Valley often painted the use of its commercial vehicle in small grey lettering. Luton-bodied Ford Transit 46 was allocated to Reading for Route Servicing, duties that included the maintenance of bus stops and timetables. New in April 1978, this vehicle would be renumbered 1089 when the company's service fleet gained four-digit numbers in June 1978. (G. Bubb)

Alder Valley 72 (OCS 597H), Reading Garage

Former Western SMT Bristol VRT had become Alder Valley 889 with the exchange of Scottish Bus Group VRTs for NBC FLFs. Retained for driver training, it is in an attractive red and yellow scheme and numbered 72. The company had renumbered its service fleet again in the September 1982, reverting to two-digit numbers.

Bristol W172, t/p 109 MR, and 2079, Swindon Garage, *c.* 1979

Bristol Omnibus' Swindon garage had been allocated a number of recovery vehicles during the NBC years. In the early 1970s, AEC Matador W141 with London Transport-style bodywork performed duties from the North Wiltshire garage. It was replaced in late 1978 by W172, a Leyland Beaver former tractor unit fitted with a crane and ballast weight. W172 is seen at its home garage in the orange livery that the company used on many service vehicles in the 1970s. It was transferred to Lawrence Hill in 1981, when Swindon garage gained converted Bristol MW recovery vehicle W151.

Bristol W151, t/p 786 HT, Gloucester Bus Station

Bristol converted three Bristol MW former coaches to recovery vehicles. W151 was converted in October 1974 from bus 2111 (404 LHT). The three conversions were transferred between garages. W151, seen here in Gloucester, would end its time at Swindon in the Cheltenham & Gloucester fleet, carrying Swindon & District NBC style fleet name. In its time as a recovery vehicle it had carried all-over NBC green, orange/white and finally yellow liveries.

Cheltenham & Gloucester RV1, t/p 109 MR, Swindon Garage

Swindon's final recovery vehicles as part of the NBC was this unusual DAF lorry. Probably a former tractor unit, it carried the number RV1 along with the longstanding local trade plates 109 MR. Note the phone number advertising its availably for commercial use. Bristol was divided into two companies by 1983. Here the local buses were in poppy red and carried Swindon & District fleet names. Note the Bristol Country Bus (Badgerline) Leyland Nationals in the background.

Bristol W120 (OHY 965), Lawrence Hill, Bristol

Former Bristol K bus C8108 of 1953 was converted to tree lopper W120 in 1967. Carrying the Bristol service vehicle orange livery, it is seen at Bristol Lawrence Hill Workshops in the 1970s. Amazingly it would be transferred to the Cheltenham & Gloucester fleet in 1983 (in yellow livery), making it one of the oldest surviving vehicles in the NBC.

Bristol W148 (280 ECY), Lawrence Hill Garage, 14 October 1973

Formerly dual-purpose 2136 was a Bristol MW of 1963, starting service with United Welsh. Coming to Bristol Omnibus in November 1964, it served as a coach until August 1973 when it was downgraded to dual purpose status. It served as a recruitment office between November 1973 and February 1974, when it reverted to PSV use briefly until sale in August the same year. This rare view sees it carrying its local coach livery with the addition of suitable lettering.

Bristol W160 (431 FHW)

In a natural progression, Bristol moved from using Bristol Ks to Bristol LDs for its trainers in the mid-1970s. Previously the company had used a cream and orange livery for its trainer fleet, but adopted this dark blue livery, very similar to Eastern National, around the same time. W160 was a Bristol LD6G and was converted in March 1976, lasting until May 1979 in its new role.

Bristol 191 (OHT 643M), Swindon Bus Station

New in April 1974, 191 was a Ford Transit 17 cwt van. It was allocated new to the electricians at Lawrence Hill Central Works. Previously Bristol had used Morris 1000 and JU vans, but it favoured Morris Marina and Ford Transit vans in the NBC years. (G. Bubb)

Bristol 95 (NFB 845Y), Lawrence Hill Garage

Bristol only published details of service vehicles that were formerly PSVs in its official fleet lists, so information on its commercial vehicles relied on enthusiasts' observations. Large Ford Transit van 95 carries the City Line lettering used by Bristol buses operating local service in the City of Bristol, though it was more usual to see CITYBUS fleet names during the end of the NBC era. (G. Bubb)

Bristol NCR 401G

Bristol operated two 'Mobile Sales Caravans', one each at Bristol and Gloucester. In 1969 it purchased NCR 401G, a BMC 250JU van for such duties. The company also used a towed caravan for such work.

Bristol 189 (NAE 502L)

A later generation of Mobile Sales Caravan was Ford Transit 189 (NAE 501L). New in June 1973, it was listed as a Marconi Control bus location system van, supporting the company's electronic bus location and control system, which was fitted to posts in Bristol City and read by a fitment on the bus roof. After its use maintaining this system the company modified it for use as a mobile ticket sales office, carrying a similar livery to NCR 401G, seen above.

Crosville G127 (KFM 776), Warrington Bank Quay, February 1974

Three Bristol L5G towing vehicles survived into the corporate NBC era. G127 was formerly bus SLG 127 and was converted in the mid-1960s. The majority of seats were removed and a simple tow bar fitment was added. Allocated to Liverpool garage, it survived until September 1976, but never received corporate fleet names.

Crosville L930 (MUH 195), Aberystwyth Garage, 1975

In 1972 Crosville took over some of the operation of Western Welsh in West Wales, three garages and a number of vehicles that were non-standard to Crosville. MUH 195 was a Leyland bus with Weymann bodywork (WWOC 1146). It became Crosville STL 930, but after a short time it became towing bus L930 for Aberystwyth garage. It was replaced by a Bristol MW conversion in autumn 1975.

Crosville G950 (286 HFM), Birkenhead Woodside Ferry Terminal, September 1978

Rock Ferry's garage (near Birkenhead) towing vehicle conversion G950 in February 1977 was an unusual as it was former Bristol Lodekka DLG 950. The use of a double-decker as a towing vehicle without being reduced to single deck was rare. This vehicle survived into the late 1980s, and was modified to allow tree cutting duties and painted white. This vehicle survives in preservation as open-top DLG 950.

Crosville G881 (838 AFM), Crewe, June 1979

Crosville's G881 was typical of the Crosville driver training fleet. DLG 881 had been allocated to Crewe when in PSV use. It was converted in the late 1970s for its new use and remained allocated to Crewe. Fortunately, it survives in preservation.

Cumberland T1 (NRM 372), Workington

Cumberland T1 was a Bristol LS6G (ex-bus 224/1275/275) was used by the company as a driver training bus from 1971. It carried NBC local coach livery until 1976, when it became a mobile office and received all-over white livery. Cumberland sold it in March 1980.

Cumberland ED5, t/p 059 RM, Whitehaven Garage, mid-1970s

Cumberland only owned two heavy recovery vehicles throughout the NBC era. The first, an AEC Matador allocated number ED5, was rebuilt in this unique style by the company. It was withdrawn in 1979 and replaced by a Leyland Bison twin boom three-axle lorry. (J. Harrington)

East Kent EK999, t/p 116 FN

Like Cumberland, East Kent only required the use of one heavy recovery vehicle. They owned an AEC Matador, which was withdrawn in 1974, and its replacement was a 1954 ex-Army Scammell Explorer, unique in the NBC. It was numbered P151 in the joint East Kent/Maidstone & District numbering scheme, but it also carried EK999. Withdrawal came in 1982. (G. Bubb)

East Kent P188, t/p 116 FN

East Kent replaced its superannuated Scammel Explorer with a more usual AEC Mandator in 1981. It was secondhand from Gulf Oil (SMU 169N) and dated from 1974. Fitted with International Wreckers Twin Boom recovery equipment, it was very similar to the Maidstone & District and London Country examples. P188 was allocated to Canterbury and Herne Bay garages. Listing also show it was also briefly with Maidstone & District in 1983. (G. Bubb)

East Kent P150 (PFN 863)

East Kent and Maidstone & District shared its training fleet, and many carried joint fleet names. P150 was a 1959 AEC Regent V with Park Royal bodywork converted in 1976. Though it carries only East Kent names, it spent some time with Maidstone & District in 1982 at Luton (Chatham) garage.

East Midland T1 (915 MRB), Chesterfield Garage

East Midland T1 was a Bristol FS6G converted to its training role in October 1977. A 1961 Bristol Lodekka with ECW H33/27RD bodywork originally with Midland General, it was transferred to Mansfield District in 1968 as 600. From 1972 it was with East Midland, numbered B600 (B300 in 1975), illustrating the complex NBC vehicle histories in this part of the East Midlands. It was withdrawn in 1985.

East Midland T2 (PNN 194F), Derby Bus Station

East Midland contrasted its trainer fleet by painting them in red – in the case of Atlantean T2, a deep non-standard shade of red. The bus fleet livery had become NBC green in 1972, losing its historic red fleet livery. T2 (PNN 194F) had become a trainer in August 1983. It was formerly bus D194, new in 1968.

East Yorkshire t/p 153 AT, Hull Paragon Station

Believed to bought in 1974, little is known about East Yorkshire's first AEC Matador. It was used from Bridlington garage, retained its original cab but received a new rear cabin and 4-ton crane. It was replaced in 1980 by the secondhand former South Wales Transport AEC Matador. (J. Harrington)

East Yorkshire UEM 320M, Hull Garage

Seen in the late 1980s, East Yorkshire ex-tractor unit ERF was bought by the company for use from its Hull garage. In NBC days it carried trade plate 270 AT and had a yellow cab and red, white and blue rear bodywork. It lasted into the privatised era, when the picture was taken in the company's new livery.

East Yorkshire CKH 780C

One of the smaller NBC constituents, East Yorkshire had a small service fleet. CKH 780C was its training vehicle in the early 1980s. An AEC Renown with Park Royal bodywork, it was new in 1965. Numbered 780, it carried the short-lived NBC blue livery in the mid-1970s. East Yorkshire sold it in 1988 to Southern Vectis for continued use as a driver trainer. Though it travelled south, Southern Vectis never put it into use.

Eastern Counties X38, t/p 591 PW, Surrey Street Garage, Norwich

In the NBC era Eastern Counties only had one heavy recovery vehicle. Until 1977 it was AEC Matador X38 (t/p 591 PW), purchased in 1959 and rebuilt by the company with stylish contemporary bodywork and a 2-ton crane. In December 1977 it was replaced by a Ford D twin boom recovery lorry, which would serve until 1992.

Eastern Counties X65 (NAG 585G), Norwich Showground, 1981

Eastern Counties X65 was a Bristol VRT new to Western SMT in October 1969 (2264). It was part of the Scottish Bus Exchange, for NBC Bristol FLFs, coming to Eastern Counties in July 1973 (VR330). It was converted to a driver trainer in June 1981. It finished its NBC service as a crew vehicle at Lowestoft bus station in 1986.

Eastern Counties X63 (FVF 422C)

Eastern Counties X63 (FVF 422C) was a Bristol FS6G converted from bus LFS122 in December 1976. It lasted until September 1982. Visible in the background is an Eastern Counties caravan. This one was based on a domestic caravan but the company also owned a large twin-axle version that could be towed by one of the Bristol FS recovery vehicles.

Eastern Counties X76 (PNG 400W), Norwich Bus Station, January 1984

The use of a BMC FG light lorry was not common in the NBC. Northern General and Midland Red operated several, while South Wales, Hants & Dorset and United all had small numbers. Eastern Counties service fleet in the NBC era contained mainly Ford commercial products – Escorts, Transit and D series were all used. X76 is seen in Norwich bus station in the early 1980s. (G. Bubb)

Eastern National 0101, t/p 572 VX, Eastern Counties Central Works, Norwich, c. 1973

Seen at neighbouring Eastern Counties Central Workshops in Norwich is Eastern National AEC Matador 0101, still in pre-NBC livery but with corporate lettering. Eastern National owned two AEC Matadors. 0101, seen here, used ECW Queen Mary coach parts, while the other, 0102, used newer parts again from ECW. Matador 0101 was transferred to Crosville in July 1984 (60A). It survives preserved in NBC yellow livery.

Eastern National 0538 (538 HVX), Southend Garage

0538 (538 HVX) was formerly Bristol LD5G 2478 and was converted in 1974. Painted in the blue livery with large red lettering, typical of Eastern National trainers at the time, it was withdrawn in late 1977.

Eastern National 9002/9008/9010, Colchester Garage

Four Eastern National driver trainers are seen parked at Colchester: 9002 (81 TVX), 9008 (RHK 347D), 9010 (RHK 346D) and one unidentified – all converted from Bristol Lodekka FLFs. 9002 was formerly bus 1572 and was converted in March 1977, while 9008/10 were converted later in 1979. It is interesting to compare this livery with the Bristol Omnibus trainer seen earlier.

Hants & Dorset 9079 (REL 743H)

Hants & Dorset 9079 was originally bus 1622, new in 1969. It was unusual in that it was a dual-door Bristol LH. It was converted for use in Market Analysis Project (MAP) studies in May 1978, becoming a towing vehicle soon after in April 1979 for use from Southampton garage. In February 1983 it moved to Eastern Counties (X82), reverting to use as a publicity unit with Ambassador Travel.

Hants & Dorset 9081 (OVX 658K), Salisbury Garage, 17 March 1979

New in October 1971, Salisbury's Ford D recovery 9081 was bought by Hants & Dorset in 1978, probably originally a tractor unit. Sometime after this photo was taken the company added a crew cab joined behind the existing Ford cab. 9081 survived with Wilts & Dorset and was out of use at Salisbury garage in 1988, being replaced by a Volvo F12 (XAG 222S) also numbered 9081. Wilts & Dorset bought another Ford D, a former cement mixer with twin rear axles: 9083 (EEW 702V) for use at Poole during its last years as a NBC company. (D. Mant)

Hants & Dorset 9050 (PRW 18M), Barton Park, Eastleigh, 7 February 1982

Tractor units were unusual in the NBC, although a few existed usually to move fuel tankers, such as with Crosville and Bristol. Hants & Dorset operated a single example: 9050, a Guy 'Big J4T' tractor unit. New in January 1974, it was bought secondhand around 1980. The company owned two articulated trailers for use with 9050: a flatbed (8050) for driver training and a tanker (7050). All were allocated to the Central Workshops at Barton Park, located in the former railway workshops at Eastleigh. (D. Mant)

Hants & Dorset 9092 (OHR 919), Eastleigh, 4 October 1980

Hants & Dorset reused its 90xx service fleet numbers. The next generation of driver trainers after Bristol KSWs were Bristol LDs. The second use of number 9092 (the first was a Bristol K) is seen at Eastleigh Workshops in 1980. It was formerly bus 428, converted in September 1976 for use at Poole garage. It was withdrawn in May 1981.

Wilts & Dorset 9077 (ORU 532M), 18 October 1988

After Hants & Dorset was divided in 1983, the newly formed Wilts & Dorset converted a Bristol LH in February 1983 from bus 3532, an unusual conversion as a former double-deck vehicle was normally the starting point for a tree cutter.

Hants & Dorset 9052 (AFH 529T), Swanage Bus Station

Hants & Dorset Bedford CF 9052 is seen in the prescribed livery for service vehicles as directed by the National Bus Company. Guidance allowed for the NATIONAL identity but no allowance for a local fleet name, though vehicles carried the legal lettering as PSVs did. 9052 was allocated to Bournemouth Holdenhurst Road garage in 1981. Hants & Dorset purchased two Bedford CF pick-ups, the other being 9060 (NAA 216P) at Southampton. (Chris Richardsen)

Wilts & Dorset 9051 (B864 OFX), Poole Bus Station

Wilts & Dorset 9051 only carries its legal lettering and fleet number to indicate its ownership. Purchased by Wilts & Dorset in August 1984 for use by the Traffic Department at Poole, when split from Hants & Dorset in 1983 the new Wilts & Dorset service fleet commercial vehicles were made up of Leyland Sherpa vans (two), Bedford CF pick-ups (two), Metro vans (two) and a Talbot express van (one). (G. Bubb)

Wilts & Dorset Salisbury 9079 (DPR 944Y), Salisbury Garage, January 1990

Talbot van 9079 still carries it NBC style fleet names, though the logo has been removed by January 1990. In use from Salisbury garage, it had replaced a secondhand large Ford Transit van, which had carried the same livery and fleet name in the high position. Wilts & Dorset started to use its post-NBC red and black livery on its service vans soon after.

Shamrock & Rambler 3199 (CDL 479C), Holdenhurst Road, Bournemouth

Shamrock & Rambler obtained former Southern Vectis Bristol FLF (611) for use as its trainer vehicle in June 1984. At this time the NBC was dividing up large fleets so there was a necessity for new companies to introduce their own support vehicles. 3199 returned to the Isle of Wight after only two years to form part of Southern Vectis' 'Vintage Fleet'. Today it can be found at the Isle of Wight Bus & Coach Museum.

Provincial T1 (HWO 344), Salisbury Garage, 12 June 1974

Gosport & Fareham traded as Provincial and was closely associated with Hants & Dorset, as seen here at Salisbury garage. As the smallest NBC constituent fleet, its service fleet consisted of a recovery lorry (a Ford Thames, then a Ford D, later replaced by at Volvo), a small open lorry (BMC JU, later a Leyland Sherpa) and a trainer bus. At the start of the corporate era it was this elderly Duple-bodied Guy Arab III, which had come from Red & White in 1967 (new in 1949 as L1949). Provincial numbered it 9 but relegated it to trainer duties as T1 in December 1970. T1 was replaced in 1975 by former City of Oxford AEC Regent V, number 60 (972 CWL). (D. Mant)

SERVICE VEHICLES 1981

Fleet No:	Reg No:	Make and Type	Chassis Type	First Lic'd	Body	Allocated to
9050	PBW 18M	Guy B.J.4.T.	JT2013B Flat Bed Trailer (8050)	1/74	Tractor Unit and Tanker (7050)	CBW
9051						
9052	AFB 529T	Bedford Lorry	97360H7626091	9/78	Pick Up Van	Holdenhurst Road Bournemouth
9053	AOD 407T	Leyland Marina	49927M	11/78	Van	Poole
9054						
9055	JAA 133S	Leyland Sherpa	ZCPABJ/051371N	4/78	Van	Salisbury
9056	JHO 31S	Leyland Sherpa	ZCHABK/052033N	6/78	Pick Up	CBW (Stores)
9058	JAA 132S	Leyland Sherpa	ZCPABJ/051370N	4/78	Van	Salisbury
9059						
9060	NAA 216F	Bedford CF	EY609275	8/75	Pick up Van	Grosvenor Square
9061	HAA 815S	Leyland 850	XKV1/519291A	4/78	Mini Van	Salisbury Traffic Inspectors
9062	HAA 812S	Leyland 850	XKV1/478230H	3/78	Mini Van	Basingstoke Traffic Inspectrs
9063						
9064	HAA 814S	Leyland 850	XKv1/194886A	3/78	Mini Van	Southampton Traffic Inspectors
9065	BHU 190T	Austin Morris 850	XKV1/572651A	3/79	Mini Van	Poole Traffic Inspectors
9066	XPX 73V	Leyland Sherpa 250	ZHPFL58N/91366	9/79	Van	Poole
9067	XPX 76V	Leyland Sherpa "	ZHPFL18N/91360	9/79	Van	Salisbury
9068	XRV 551V	Leyland Sherpa "	ZHPFL18N/93359	10/79	Van	CBW
9069	KOM 811P	Ford Escort 1100	BBAVHT38479	11/75	Van	Southampton Publicity
9079	REL 743E	Bristol LH6L	LH300	10/69	Towing Vehicle	Grosvenor Square
9080	DCG 984S	Leyland Terrier	517695	8/77	Dropside Truck	CBW (Stores)
9081	OVX 685K	Ford Tractor Unit	51666	10/71	Recovery Crane	Salisbury (Trade Plates)
9082	Trade P	Atkinson Tanker	FC 9559	12/63	RecoveryVeh	Holdenhurst Rd B'mouth
9084	Trade Plates	AEC Matador	O6530557	-/60	Recovery Crane	Grosvenor Square
9085	Trade Plates	Bedford 6 Ton	10667	-	Recovery Crane	Basingstoke
9086	GFN 801	Bristol LH6gB	13829B	6/59	Tree Cutter	Poole
9087	NLJ 52DN	Bristol LH6L	LH894	2/74	Recovery Vehicle	Poole
9088	REL 745E	Bristol LH6L	302	9/69	Towing Vehicle	CBW
9089	ECG 359N	Leyland Terrier	479943	4/75	Dropside Truck	CBW (Stores)

1 June 1981

Hants & Dorset Service Fleet, 1981

Hants & Dorset published fleet lists. Fortunately they included details of all service vehicles and even staff cars. Here is the 1981 service fleet. Numbers 9001–9049 were allocated to staff cars, though the company's Hillman Husky vans were painted yellow, carried fleet names and were numbered in the car series. 9050–9089, shown here, were allocated to recoveries, lorries, vans and miscellaneous vehicles. Trainers were numbered 9090 onwards, though the company later used 92xx numbers.

Lincolnshire 11, t/p 134 FE

Lincolnshire bought two ex-government AEC Matadors, which were rebuilt with near identical bodywork. Using elements of ECW Queen Mary coach panels, they were allocated to Lincoln (11) and Scunthorpe (12). Neither carried a crane as they were towing vehicles only, and both were replaced in the mid-1970s. Lincoln received an Ergomatic Leyland rebuilt by the company and Scunthorpe received another AEC Matador, former United 45/68. Both lasted into privatisation.

Lincolnshire 6, t/p 419 FE, Scunthorpe Garage, March 1986

Lincolnshire replacement recovery at Scunthorpe was another AEC Matador, formerly with United, who had rebuilt it with Bristol RE parts as late as June 1974. Strangely United replaced it with a Ford D soon after in 1977/8. Repainted from poppy red into this yellow/green livery, it survived into the 1990s with Roadcar. (G. Bubb)

Lincolnshire 9 (9322 PT), Newark Garage

Former Northern General Leyland Atlantean 3170 was converted for use in the Market Analysis Project work. In this guise it was used by a number of companies including Lincolnshire, Yorkshire Traction and West Riding/Yorkshire, retaining this livery but changing the fleet name. Lincolnshire fitted it with fleet plate 9 in its service fleet series, which it retained while in use with the other constituents. Converted in February 1979, it was withdrawn in March 1983.

Lincolnshire 10 (OFW 801), Skegness Garage

Lincolnshire converted Bristol SC 2604 for use as a mobile travel office in March 1978, but when seen at Skegness it was in use for Left Luggage. Lincolnshire later converted a Bristol RE coach for use as a replacement mobile travel office similar in 8/80 from coach 1404, a more extensive modification with a roller door on the side and several windows sealed.

London Country 583J, t/p 6959P, Garston Garage

Soon after it was transferred into the NBC, London Country purchased two Matadors. The second was 583J, allocated to Reigate and Garston garages, which was purchased in March 1972. Retaining most of its original bodywork, it was withdrawn in March 1979. The other Matador 582J is featured in the first volume of this series. (J. Harrington)

London Country M1, t/p 6433P, Stevenage Garage

London Country purchased two AEC Ergomatics in 1976 from International Wreckers to supplement its existing AEC Matadors (582/3J). M1 (UNO 205E) was new in 1967. Based at Garston (Watford) and Hemel Hempstead garages, it lasted into privatisation when it passed to London Country North West (LCNW). The other Mandator (also listed as a Mercury) was M2 (new in 1969), which was allocated to Romford, Northfleet and Dartford garages, and then passed to LCSE.

London Country M4, t/p 6431P, Hertford Garage, 31 March 1986

After London Country purchased a third AEC Mandator (M3) for Reigate garage in July 1980, its next heavy recovery lorry was a secondhand Leyland Marathon from Blue Circle Cement, in September 1982. Initially it had all-over yellow livery. It was only ever allocated to Hertford garage, numbered M4, on trade plate 6421P. With the privatisation split of the company, each of the four heavy recovery lorries went to one of the newly formed geographic companies. M4 passed to London Country North East (LCNE).

London Country RF556 (NLE 556), Romford, 3 June 1976

London Country converted three of its famous AEC Regal 'RFs' to towing buses. RF556 (NLE 556) was converted in January 1973 and allocated to Hertford garage. When London Country was formed from the County area of London Transport, it received no dedicated recovery vehicles. RF556 and RF594 were converted to supplement the company's two AEC Matadors, which were purchased secondhand in 1971.

London Country RF79 (LYF 430), Leatherhead Garage, 5 April 1980

London Country gained a third 'RF' towing vehicle in October 1978. This time they used a coach version for the conversion. RF79 retained its PSV fleet number, as did the majority of the company's former bus conversions. Allocated to Leatherhead garage, by 1980 it was out of use, though it did pass into preservation in East Anglia.

London Country 17A (TPD 893M), Lingfield

Photographs of London Country's earlier vans are rare. In 1972/3 the company purchased five BLMC J4 vans, 4/5/6A and 16/17A, along with several Ford Transit 75 vans. Initially some were in grey livery similar to London Transport service vehicles, but later they gained NBC green livery. All were withdrawn in 1978, though 16A remained listed until 1980. 17A was allocated to Swanley garage.

London Country 15F (GPK 515N), Reigate, 1 April 1975

London Country's Ford A 5-ton open lorry 15F (GPK 515N) is seen passing Reigate garage in 1975. New in April 1973, it was withdrawn in September 1980. The Ford A was a rare vehicle in NBC service use, with West Riding and Midland Red known to have examples.

London Country 1241F (965 ELR)

London Country gained twelve Ford Thames Trader lorries from London Transport in 1970. Four were specially designed for tree pruning (1241–1244F) – five were built but London Transport retained one for its own use. All four tree pruning vehicles were withdrawn in August 1979, though two bodies were transferred to new Ford D chassis (34/35F) to continue performing these duties.

London Country 14F (RPB 933L), Addlestone Garage, 13 April 1980

Though London Country used Austin and Bedford vans, the majority were Ford Transits. The company operated thirty-six between 1971 and 1986. 14F, seen at Addlestone garage in 1980, is typical of the type in LCBS use. New in April 1973, it was withdrawn soon after the photograph was taken, in September 1980.

Maidstone & District P30, t/p 071 KJ

Maidstone & District rebuilt its two AEC Matadors (E1/E2) with near identical bodywork, incorporating a completely new cab and work area, with the later style AEC grill. In 1973 they were renumbered E1 to P30 and E2 to P31. P30 was bought in 1959 from the War Department and allocated to Gillingham garage. Both were repainted in chrome yellow in the late 1970s, and were withdrawn in 1982, though both were preserved. (G. Bubb)

Maidstone & District P35. t/p 071 KJ

In 1979 Maidstone & District purchased two secondhand AEC Mandators (P34/P35). Both were ex-Gulf Oil, new in 1971 (P34) and 1972 (P35). They were rebuilt with International Wreckers twin boom equipment. Gillingham's P35, seen here recovering a Bristol VR, was originally registered MMK 502L. Near identical P34 was allocated to Tunbridge Wells. Both survived into privatisation in 1986. (G. Bubb)

East Kent/Maidstone & District P160 (MFN 946F)

Though part of the East Kent fleet, AEC Regent P160 (MFN 946F), converted to a mobile sales unit in 1978, was on loan to Maidstone & District. Renumbered P164 in 1979, in common with many other ex-PSV service vehicles in the two fleets, it carries both East Kent and Maidstone & District names. With the division of Maidstone & District it went to Hastings & District, who painted it blue and yellow for use as a driver trainer. After withdrawal it was preserved as part of Stagecoach's Heritage fleet in original East Kent red and cream livery.

Maidstone & District P56 (MKN 119P), Chatham (Luton) Garage, February 1978

P56, a Ford Transit 75 van, was new in 1976. A long-term resident of Chatham (Luton) garage, it survived until 1984, a comparatively long time for a NBC commercial vehicle. Maidstone & District used this livery for many of its vans.

Midland Red M153, t/p 517 DA, Digbeth Garage, Birmingham

Midland Red bought two AEC Matadors from the War Department in 1947. For some time both operated with the original cab and bodywork. M153, seen here, was rebuilt in 1962 using parts similar to the Midland Red motorway coaches. The other Matador, M268, was also rebuilt but lacked the distinctive windscreen seen above. M153 passed to Midland Red (West) and then into the privatised company, gaining registration Q142 VOE. It was then sold to Birmingham Busways, who used it until 2007, making it the last Matador in PSV service use in the country. It is preserved in the West Midlands.

Midland Red 4761, t/p 371 HA, Shrewsbury Garage

Recently converted BMMO D7 towing conversion 4761 is seen at its home garage of Shrewsbury. From 1972 the company converted eleven D7 double-deck buses to towing vehicles. All were reduced to single deck but with a variety of styles of bodywork finishing. Three converted at Wigston had full length bodies, while the rest had open platforms. 4761 was converted at Shrewsbury garage in March 1973, in its chosen style retaining one bay. Those at Malvern retained two bays, apart from 4494, which had one and a half. From 1977, the D7 conversions were replaced by nine LC9 coach conversion, all of which were identical and cut back to one bay. The final D7 conversion was withdrawn in January 1981. 4761 was withdrawn in August 1980.

Midland Red 5517 (6517 HA), 2225 (SBF 233), Heath Hayes Garage, May 1977

Two Midland Red driver trainers are seen at the former Harper Brothers garage at Heath Hayes, near Cannock. 5517 (6517HA) was a formerly a S16 bus, and 2225 (SBF 233) was a Leyland PD2 that had come from Harper Brothers with the takeover in 1974. It continued as a PSV until February 1976, when it became a training vehicle. In 1981 it was rebuilt as a towing vehicle, reduced to single deck with an open rear platform. By the time it was completed Midland Red and been split in four, and it entered service with Midland Red North at Wellington garage. 2225 survives preserved in NBC yellow.

BDJ 808, t/p 413 HA, Heath Hayes Garage, 1974

Midland Red took over the operations of Harper Brothers of Heath Hayes, on Cannock Chase, in September 1974. The garage and much of the fleet was also taken into Midland Red ownership. The company had recently converted its AEC Regent (10) as its recovery vehicle. It was briefly in Midland Red ownership, but never received a repaint in NBC livery. Seen here in the yard of it home garage, it it would have looked superb in NBC yellow livery!

Midland Red 5 (JHA 21L), Birmingham City Centre, 21 August 1973

Midland Red used the BMC FG in various weights and sizes. Number 5 was a heavy variant with double rear wheels, and painted in poppy red with a grey fleet number on the door and small NBC logo. Though details of the company's towing vehicle bus conversions are well documented, little is published about Midland Red's other service vehicles in the NBC period, though some information was available after the 1981 four-way split, when some of the new companies published fleet lists.

Midland Red TOL 727S, Birmingham, 1987

The Ford A was never as common as the Transit or D type lorry on the roads in the 1970s. A few NBC constituents bought them, such as LCBS, East Kent and West Riding, but they could be reported as Ford Transits, so information is not always clear. Midland Red bought TOL 727S in 1978, which passed to Midland Red West with the September 1981 company split. It lasted until 1989 with the privatised company.

Midland Red COF 463V, Leicester, 30 May 1980

Photographs of Midland Red vans are rare. Ford Escort Mk2 van COF 463V was caught at Leicester in 1980. The company had used BMC FG open lorries at the start of the NBC era, but changed to Fords in the mid-1970s, using Escort vans and Transit vans and pick-ups. (G. Bubb)

National Welsh E2, Bulwark Central Workshop, Chepstow, 1981

National Welsh E2 (t/p 355 BO) is seen withdrawn at the company's Central Works in 1981. Western Welsh bought two ex-government AEC Matadors in February 1959, numbered V1/2. Both were rebuilt in near identical finish by the company in 1970 and renumbered to E1/2 in 1974. E1 was used from Ely, Bridgend and Cwmbran garages. E2 saw use from Neath and Cwmbran. It was withdrawn in July 1981, much earlier than E1 (which became E1051 in January 1983), which lasted until 1990 with the reformed Red & White at Brymawr on registration Q388 UHB. Both survive in preservation.

National Welsh E3, t/p 106 BO, Porth Garage

Bought in January 1971, Western Welsh's third AEC Matador was not quite as it appeared. It was rebuilt by the company with an ergonomic cab at its Ely Workshops. Numbered V3, it entered service at Porth garage. Renumbered E3 in 1974 and E1052 in 1983, it was withdrawn by 1985.

Western Welsh E4, t/p 026 BO, Crosskey Garage, 1977

E4 was converted in November 1977. The conversions were straightforward with the removal of most seats and a towing point fitted to the rear. E4 was converted from U561 (365 BAX), which became E1053 in 1983. It was withdrawn in August 1985.

National Welsh E5 (DAX 605C), Bulwark Central Workshop, Chepstow, 1981

The fleet number E5 was used twice by Western Welsh/National Welsh, firstly for Bristol MW towing conversion of bus U358 (TWO 67) in July 1975, which carried Red & White NBC fleet names. It was withdrawn in October 1979. The second use of E5 is seen above during the final stages of conversion at Bulwark Workshops. Formerly bus U265 (DAX 605C), it was completed in November 1981. Renumbered E1054 in 1983, it was allocated to Chepstow garage, which was adjacent to the Central Workshops. It survived until February 1991 with the privatised Red & White.

Jones E6, t/p 259 AX, Bulwark Central Workshop, Chepstow

The Western Welsh group/National Welsh converted eleven Bristol MWs to towing vehicles. E6, seen here, was converted from bus U161 in 1978, for use from Abergeeg garage, carrying the Jones fleet name. E6 became E1055 in the January 1983 renumbering scheme. It was withdrawn in September 1985.

National Welsh E7, t/p 243 BO, Bulwark Central Workshop, Chepstow

Bristol MW bus U1258 (TWO 76) was converted in December 1977 for use at Barry garage. It is seen at the company's Central Workshops being towed by another former Bristol MW. E7 carried both registrations AAX 305A and AAX 383A from March 1986. It was withdrawn in 1987.

National Welsh E8, t/p 357 BO, Penarth Road Garage, Cardiff

E8 was Western Welsh's second Bristol MW conversion, completed in November 1976 from bus U1758 (TWO 81). Renumbered E1057 in 1983, it was withdrawn in April 1985.

National Welsh E22, t/p 395 BO, Bridgend Garage

E22 (later E1059), ex-U2058 (TWO 84), was looking a bit tired when photographed outside its garage in Bridgend. Converted in April 1977, it would be another vehicle used to carry a cherished plate, in this case AAX 286A from January 1986.

National Welsh E1058 (TKG 518J), Cross Keys Garage, April 1991

After using Bristol MW for towing bus conversions, the company chose Leyland Leopards for its next conversions. Ten were selected for conversion but only five were completed by December 1985. E1058 was former U1272. The NBC was privatised soon after and this vehicle went to the new Red & White company. It survives in preservation.

National Welsh E1077 (BTX 332J), Cwmbran Garage, 18 January 1988

E1077 was originally Western Welsh 2332 (U1280), but had been ordered by Rhondda Transport. Converted in 1985 to a towing vehicle, after 1986 it passed to the new Red & White company at Cwmbran garage, surviving long enough to become RW2 with Stagecoach.

National Welsh E1086 (TKG 506J), Bulwark Central Workshop, Chepstow

E1086 had the honour of being the last towing conversion undertaken by National Welsh before it was privatised in 1986. Formerly UD1287, the cutting down to one bay and an open rear platform made this conversion unique within National Welsh. Seen while undergoing conversion at Bulwark in 1984, it was allocated to Barry garage. It survived until 1992 with Rhondda Buses.

National Welsh E1086 (TKG 506J), Barry Garage

E1086 is seen completed at its home garage in Barry. It had briefly carried a NBC logo. National Welsh had been formed in 1978, from Western Welsh (the Rhondda name had already been discontinued), Red & White and Jones, though the Jones names continued for a short time. After its privatisation in 1988, National Welsh had a torturous existence, ceasing to exist as soon as 1992. The few surviving service vehicles were in poor external condition, very much a feature of bus operations at the time.

National Welsh T5 (16 FAX)

Western Welsh/National Welsh had a relatively small training fleet, using PSVs at temporary trainers until 1977 when it allocated L2060 a Bristol FL6G (renumbered as T1, later T1063) to a permanent training vehicle. T5 was converted in July 1979 from bus L4162, it served until August 1985. A small mix of Bristol FLs and MWs, Leyland Leopards, Leyland PDR1 and even a single Leyland National would all be painted yellow and allocated for driver tuition.

National Welsh E9 (SKG 893S), Bulwark Central Workshop, Chepstow

National Welsh purchased a number of Leyland 440EAs with Asco bodywork for rural services. Two passed into service use in December 1981, E9 (ex MD1977) and E25 (ex MD1377), both of which were publicity vehicles. E9 is seen at the National Welsh CRW in Bulwark, recently repainted. In January 1983 they were renumbered to P1071 (E9) and P1072 (E25), although they were withdrawn in March 1983 so may not have carried the new numbers.

Western Welsh 9 (OUH 159G), 9 July 1970

Seen when nearly new, BMC 700FG open lorry was one of a pair, (V) 9 new in February 1969 and 10 (SBO 911H) of March 1970. Both served in the NBC corporate era until 1979. Number 9, seen above, was later painted all over white and received a NBC logo on the door.

National Welsh E1079 (OTX 703R), Bulwark Central Workshop, Chepstow

Leyland Terrier open lorry E1079 was new in February 1977 as E21. Western Welsh had two Leyland Terriers. The other was E16 (WTG 306T), new in January 1979. E1079 is seen undergoing repair work at the company's central repair workshop.

National Welsh E1079 (OTX 703R), Bulwark Central Workshop, Chepstow

E1079 is seen again soon afterwards nearing completion. This lorry was listed as sold by October 1985. Interestingly the other Leyland Terrier (E16), by then E1078, was sold to neighbouring South Wales Transport in October 1984 and numbered 47 by its new owner.

National Welsh E1062 (B44 YWO), Bulwark Central Workshop, Chepstow September 1984

E1062, a Bedford TL1260 open lorry, was new to National Welsh in August 1984. Seen when brand new, it was the last lorry the company would purchase as a state-owned company. With privatisation it stayed at the CRW site with the newly formed Bulwark Engineering.

National Welsh E1099 (A208 XWO), Bulwark Central Workshop, Chepstow, May 1984

National Welsh bought two Bedford CF35D light lorries in May 1984. The company fitted them out with Luton bodies at the Bulwark CRW, and both were painted in the same scheme. E1099 was allocated to Cwmbran garage, while E1098 went to Bridgend. With privatisation E1099 would eventually pass to Red & White.

Red & White E27 (HAX 822L), Bulwark Central Workshop, Chepstow

Ford Transit HAX 822L is seen in 1973 with its original lettering. In August 1974 it became E27 with Western Welsh. It served from the Central Workshop until withdrawn in December 1983. Note R&W Ford Trader 530E lorry 905 CAX parked alongside.

Red & White E28 (OWO 669M), Bulwark Central Workshop, Chepstow

Red & White owned a single van when it became part of the NBC. It was Ford Escort Mk 1 van registered OWO 669M, new in 1973. It also passed to Western Welsh in August 1974 and was numbered E28. It would last until July 1983, and was renumbered E1077 in January 1983.

Western Welsh 14 (MAX 325P), Bulwark Garage, Chepstow

Western Welsh, Red & White and Jones only used Ford Escorts for its small van throughout the NBC era. Ford Escort Mk2 van 14, devoid of its E prefix, was new in March 1976. Renumbered E1073 by National Welsh, it was sold in October 1983.

Red & White E14 (MAX 325P)

E14 is seen again, though lettered for Red & White. The name Red & White had returned to National Welsh in the early 1980s for operations in the eastern parts of South Wales.

REG NO.	MAKE	TYPE	CHASSIS NO.	COMPANY LORRIES					
				YEAR	FIRST LICENCED	BODY TYPE	ALLOCATION	VAN NO.
(TP) 358 BO	AEC	Matador	08539584			Closed	Ely	E1
(TP) 355 BO	"	"	08537120			"	Cwmbran	E2
(TP) 129 BO	"	"	08534629			Open	Porth	E3
365 BAX	Bristol	MW6G	184169	1961	12/61	ECW	Crosskeys	E4
								E5
361 BAX	Bristol	MW6G	181103	1961	7/61	ECW	Cwmbran	E6
TWO 76	"	"	139076	1958	11/58	Bus	Barry	E7
TWO 81	"	"	139102	1958	11/58	"	Penarth Road	E8
								E9
								E10
								E11
OAX 613C	Bristol	MW6G	225052	1965	6/65	ECW	Porth	E12
MAX 325P	Ford	Escort Van	BBAV5822818	1976	3/76	Van	Chepstow Publicity	E14
UHB 81S	"	" "	BBAVTD51943	1978	1/78	"	Ely (Stores)	E15
WTG 306T	Leyland	Terrier	536661	1978	1/79	Open Drop Side	Ely	E16
YTG 377T	Ford	Escort Van	BBAVWC73009	1979	2/79	Van		E17
RBU 222F	AEC	Tanker	3447	1967	6/67	Rigid	Ely	E18
CUH 782V	Ford	Escort Van	BBAVWT90380	1979	10/79	Van	Ely	E19
TP) 010 AX	Bedford		RLW3		5/68	Open	Tredegar	E20
OTX 703R	Leyland	Terrier TR738	506041	1977	4/77	Open drop	Chepstow (Stores)	E21
TWO 84	Bristol	MW6G	139112	1958	11/58	Bus	Bridgend	E22
KWO 826E	Ford	D300C	BC01FG15392	1967	3/67	Open Drop	Chepstow (CRS)	E24
								E25
TP) 308 AX	Bedford		27552			Open	Chepstow Depot	E26
HAX 822L	Ford	Transit	BC05NJ671DBX	1973	2/73	Open Drop	Chepstow	E27
OWO 669M	"	Escort Van	BB1VHD121969	1973	/73	Van	Bridgend Publicity	E28
18 FAX	Bristol	MW6G	213078	1962	8/63	ECW	Aberdare	E29
20 AAX	"	FL	168025	1961	2/61	"	Cardiff	T1
5 AAX	"	"	168005	1961	1/61	"		T2
605 BBO	Ley.Leopard	3/2R	621609	1962	11/62	Willowbrook		T3
617 BBO	"	"	621954	1962	11/62	"		T4
16 FAX	Bristol	MW6G	195176	1962	2/62	ECW		T5
13 AAX	"	FL	168013	1960	1/61	"		T6
12 AAX	"	"	168012	1960	1/61	"		T7

National Welsh Service Vehicle Fleet List, 1981

The company's official fleet list, service vehicle page, for 1981 illustrates the variety of vehicles in use. E1–29 (no E13) was allocated to recovery/towing vehicles and commercial vehicles and T1–7 for training vehicles. The fleet was renumbered into the E10xx series, though T and P prefixes were allocated in January 1983.

Northern General 3045 (9034 PT), Sunderland Garage

Northern General cut down Leyland PDR 3045 in February 1976 for use from its Sunderland garage. Later 3045 would be repainted with the white band swept up and forward in the contemporary style from the *Starsky & Hutch* TV show! Northern General usually retained the original numbers for a bus converted to towing duties, but allocated new DTxx numbers for a training vehicle. The rest of its service fleet was numbered in a two-digit serial from 45–99.

Northern General T261 (AUP 341B), South Shields Garage

Northern General T261 retained its number from its previous driver training use, when it was cut down to a towing tender in December 1981. New in 1964 as bus 341 with Sunderland District, then 4208 with Northern, it was a Leyland Leopard PS3/1R. It became training bus DT26 (later T261) in September 1977. It continued in use with Go-Ahead Northern after privatisation.

Northern General T211 (AFT 930), Percy Main Garage, 24 June 1979

Driver trainer AFT 930 was a Leyland PD3/4 converted in February 1975 from bus 230 (Tynemouth fleet) and numbered DT21. It was renumbered T211 in January 1978, lasting in use until 1978.

Northern General T431 (GCN 845G)

2345 started life as a dual-door bus with Northern General in 1970. Converted to training duties in August 1980, it received its green livery, which the company adopted for its trainers to avoid confusion with TWPTE sponsored services, which used yellow buses. Northern General was unique within the NBC for its choice of Marshall Camair on Leyland Panther chassis. Though Midland Red had received a few from Stratford Blue, they did not enter service.

Oxford ED2, t/p 016 FC, Oxford Garage

Oxford operated an AEC Matador with its original cab until 1971 when the company bought a former LAD cabbed Leyland Comet (AFC 62C) BRS tractor unit (MB31) and rebuilt it with the crane from the Matador. Numbered ED2, the Motor Panels MkII or 'LAD' cab was rare in the NBC – only Alder Valley and Trent used them as recovery lorries, and Trent's was only briefly in the early 1970s. ED2 was sold to private bus operator Morris of Pencoed in South Wales.

Oxford ED1, t/p 016 FC, Oxford Garage

Oxford ED1 was one of the Ford D conversion undertaken by United Counties for other NBC constituents. These vehicles had a complicated history. Ten were converted from this wheelbase (two others which were longer): two for United Automobile, three for Northern General, one for West Riding/Yorkshire Woollen, four for United Counties (excluding one which was briefly used before going to United), and this single example for Oxford South Midland. ED1 was delivered to the company in December 1977. It was replaced at an unknown date by a Leyland Octopus with a 'Chinese Six' chassis, also numbered ED1. (J. Harrington)

Oxford 761 (761 MFC), Oxford Garage, September 1976

A small fleet Oxford only required a couple of training vehicles. 761 was an AEC Reliance with Marshall bodywork, which had taken up training duties in 1974 while still in Oxford traditional maroon livery with NBC fleet names. By 1976 it had been repainted in all-over yellow livery.

Oxford 339 (339 TJO), Oxford Garage

Oxford converted this AEC Renown (339) for use as a 'planning bus'. The company repainted it a number of times according to its use. Occasionally rented to Oxford District Council, whose livery it is seen in here, it was photographed on the occasion of an open day at Oxford garage where it interestingly contained a 'Photographic look at the NBC fleet'.

Oxford ED3 (GUD 883N)

For a period, Oxford painted its commercial service vehicles in plain white livery. ED3 was a Ford Escort 7cwt van, new in 1975. The addition of hand-painted advertising was usual on their vans at this time. (L. Young)

Oxford ED8 (HJO 904S), Gloucester Green Bus Station, Oxford

Oxford reused its ED fleet numbers. ED8, new in 1978, had replaced an earlier ED8 (GUD 899N), also a Ford Transit van, of 1975. Interestingly the van carries the hand-painted name 'Easy-One'. (L. Young)

Oxford ED10 (TFC 326T), Gloucester Green Bus Station, Oxford

Oxford's ED10 was a minibus. Usually these vehicles are used to ferry crews between bus stations and the local garage. The Oxford South Midland garage was some distance from the city's bus station, so the addition of this type of vehicle would make sense. ED10 was a Bedford CF new in 1979. Again the vehicle carries an advert for the company's coaching operations. (G. Bubb)

Ancillary Vehicles

ED2	T/P (016FC)	Leyland Comet breakdown truck	1965
ED3	GUD 883N	Ford Escort 7 cwt van	1975
ED4	GUD 882N	Ford Escort 7 cwt van	1975
5	NWL 114H	Ford Transit 15 cwt van (petrol)	1969
ED6	GJB 227C	Austin Gipsy	1965
ED7	KKK 715E	Bedford J1Z10 35 cwt van	1967
ED8	GUD 899N	Ford Transit 90 van	1975
ED9	GUD 873N	Ford D0607 lorry	1975

ED2   ex British Road Service tractor unit (MB31) in 1973 registration no. AFC 62C
ED6   ex South Midland (Thames Valley) No. 59 in 1971
ED7   ex Maidstone & District in 1972

Staff Cars

RFC 422J	Triumph 2000 automatic	1970
MUD 307L	Ford Escort	1973
MUD 308L	Ford Escort	1973
UBW 148L	Morris 1800	1973
XBW 662M	Austin 1300	1973
XBW 663M	Austin 1300	1973
PHA 451M	Triumph 2000 automatic	1974
HJO 770N	Austin 1800	1975

PHA 451M ex Midland Red 1974

Non-PSVs

200	200 KFC	AEC Regent V–East Lancs L-RD trainer bus built 1960	
339	339 TJO	AEC Renown–Park Royal H-F planning bus built 1964	
761	761 MFC	AEC Reliance–Marshall B-F trainer bus built 1961	

200 and 761 are painted in a yellow livery
339 is on hire to Oxford District Council as a "Planning Bus" and is in a white/blue/mauve livery

Oxford South Midland Service Vehicles, 1975

This list illustrates the small fleet of service vehicles required by the company. Both the Leyland Comet and Austin Gipsy were still in use, and the majority of commercials were Fords, many new in 1975. Also, it shows the transfer of a service vehicle from another NBC fleet: ED7, an Austin J1 van from Maidstone & District.

Potteries t/p 484 EH, Stoke Garage

Potteries Motor Traction, better known as PMT, replaced its AEC Matador with a Leyland Bison in 1976. Registered RNU 812K but carrying trade plates 484 EH, it was new in 1971. Fitted with WreckMaster twin boom equipment, it served the company as its only recovery vehicle into the privatised era, post-1986. (J. Harrington)

Potteries T3 (927 UVT), Stoke Garage

In 1978 PMT had a fleet of three driver training vehicles. T3 (927 UVT) was a 1962 Leyland Leopard that had been converted in July 1977. The other two vehicles at this time were a pair of ex-Southdown Bristol FG6G/ ECW, T1/2 (DPM 66/67C). Initially, from 1972, PMT had used a light blue livery for its trainers but had changed to a more standard yellow by the mid-1970s.

Potteries T1 (AEH 135C), Stoke Garage

After its two Bristol FG6G were withdrawn, Potteries converted one of its own vehicles to a driver trainer. 1035 was a Daimler Fleetline with Alexander body. New in 1965, it lasted into the privatised PMT fleet.

SERVICE FLEET

Fleet No.	Reg. No.	Make	New	Remarks
T1	DPM 66C	Bristol FS6G/E.C.W.	1965	*Driver Training Vehicle
T2	DPM 67C	Bristol FS6G/E.C.W.	1965	*Driver Training Vehicle
T3	927 UVT	†Leyland Leopard PSU3/3	1962	Driver Training Vehicle
—	RNU 812K	‡Leyland Bison	1971	Heavy Recovery Vehicle
—	UEH 100L	Ford Transit	1973	Van
—	UEH 101L	Ford Transit	1973	Van
—	BEH 220H	Ford Transit	1970	Pickup Truck
—	HRE 571N	Ford Transit	1975	Van
—	RRF 915R	Ford D.0710	1977	Open Lorry
—	RRF 916R	Ford D.0710	1977	Open Lorry

Acquired by PMT 11/76 ex Southdown

†Entered Service Fleet 4/77 ex SN927

‡Carries Trade Plates

Potteries Fleet List, 1978

Potteries Motor Traction was relatively a small operator. Its geographic area was centered on the Potteries conurbation, so its garages were relatively close together, therefore it had a small service fleet. In 1972 it had two recoveries, a Matador and an Austin Gypsy, but by 1978 just the Leyland Bison was sufficient.

Ribble BD1, t/p 157 CK, Preston Bus Station

Ribble's three Leyland PS2 breakdown conversions of 1965 are well known. BD1 was allocated to Preston garage, and the other two were BD2 (Bootle) and BD3 (Carlisle). All three of the Leyland PS2 conversions were saved for preservation, but BD1 was subsequently destroyed by fire.

Ribble BD1 t/p 067 CK Preston Bus Station

BD1, shown above, was replaced at Preston in the early 1980s by this Leyland Buffalo, also numbered BD1. The company had four of these recovery vehicles (BD1–4). Nearly identical, they survived into the privatised era.

Ribble TD7 (NRN 567), Preston Bus Station

TD7 was a Leyland Atlantean converted to its new role in June 1981, one of four converted in 1981 (TD5–8). TD7 is seen here performing driver instruction, departing from Preston's iconic bus station.

North Western ODB 117G, Charles Street Workshops, Stockport

ODB 117G was a Bedford TK open lorry new to North Western RCC in 1970. When North Western was divided in 1973 between Crosville, Trent and SELNEC, this lorry found itself in the Ribble fleet. It is still in NWRCC livery when photographed at its original owners' workshops in Stockport.

Southdown 0830 ,t/p 242 HC, Eastbourne Garage

To replace its four elderly Leyland TD5 open gantry recovery vehicles, Southdown purchased another AEC Matador and three Bedford SHZ former 'Green Goddess' AFS fire engines from the dealer L.W. Vass. They were converted to recovery vehicles by the removal of some bodywork and the addition of a 5T Turner crane. 0830 (NYR 459) was allocated to Eastbourne garage, while the other two went to Brighton (0829) and Portsmouth (0831). 0829 was long lasting, serving with Hampshire Bus at Winchester as late as 1990, and 0831 survives in preservation.

Southdown 0828 (TSU 352)

Southdown's second AEC Matador was purchased in April 1973 to replaced Canadian Ford 0827 at Worthing garage. 0827 was one of the last wartime Canadian Fords still in service with the NBC. It was transferred to Horsham before withdrawal in July 1974. The Matador numbered 0828 was rebuilt by the company using bus parts, unlike the company's other Matador 0826, which retained its original cab and body. 0828 is seen in preservation in its original NBC yellow livery using the registration TSU 352.

Southdown 0832, t/p 162 AP (YJB 271J), Epson Racecourse

Southdown Leyland Retriever 0832 was purchased secondhand in 1980. It would be the last recovery vehicle the company would purchase as a NBC constituent. Fitted with Wreckers International Twin Boom equipment, it was based at Conway Street, Brighton. (G. Bubb)

Southdown 0833 (DLK 292C), Eastbourne, 1985

A number of NBC constituents, including Bristol, Crosville and Midland Red, purchased fuel tankers. Southdown's AEC Mammoth Major Tanker 0833 (DLK 292C) was bought secondhand from Shell in December 1979. Seen inside the company's Eastbourne garage in 1985, this vehicle survived into preservation with a replacement cab, superbly restored in this livery.

Southdown V9 (XFG 309S)

Southdown Ford Transit van V9 was new in 1978. Also allocated to Brighton, it was used as a mobile engineering workshop. Note the other NBC constituents' names on the door – with a nationalised organisation this sort of joint assistance was possible. (G. Bubb)

Southern Vectis 004 (GXX 785), t/p 07 DL

Southern Vectis's single recovery vehicle was an AEC Matador purchased in 1963 and rebuilt by the company at its workshop in Newport. Originally painted in Tillings green livery, it was painted yellow in the corporate era. It served until 1986, after which it was saved for preservation, eventually returning to the island.

Southern Vectis 003 (WDL 464T), Newport Bus Station, October 1985

During the NBC corporate era Southern Vectis' standard livery for its commercial service vehicles was green/white. The same as the dual-purpose PSVs, initially they retained pre-1972 gold underlined serif fleet names. WDL 464T, a Morris Marina van, was new in November 1978 and lasted until October 1989.

SERVICE FLEET

001	DDL 50	Bristol K	1940	RE	Tree Cutter
002	GDL 343N	Bedford 35 CWT	1974	NT	With Crane
003	GDL 645N	Austin 7 Cwt	1975	NT	
004	GXX 785	A E C Matador	1945	NT	Breakdown Vehicle
007	ADL 705L	Bedford 8 Cwt	1973	RE	
008	NDL 58G	Bedford 10/12 Cwt	1969	NT	
009	PDL 942H	Bedford 18 Cwt	1970	NT	
010	VDL 298K	Bedford 8 Cwt	1972	SK	
013	EDL 602D	Ford Anglia Van	1966	SK	
	MDL 461G	Honda 50 Motor Cycle	1968	NT	

Southern Vectis Fleet List, August 1975

The company's official fleet list included service vehicles with allocations. Note there was no permanent driver training vehicle at this time, and there was a generous allocation of small vans. Interestingly the company had a 50cc motorcycle.

South Wales 1, t/p 518 CY, Ravenhill Garage, Swansea

South Wales Transport obtained its Matador from government surplus stock and rebuilt it at it Ravenhill Central Workshops in the Swansea suburbs. Completed in April 1958, it was painted in the dark red used by the fleet at the time. Painted white for a time, it was yellow in the 1970s, and similar to many of its other service vehicles it carried no fleet name. It was withdrawn in April 1980 when the company purchased an impressive Magirus Uranus tractor unit (ex-Swiss Army) for conversion to heavy recovery. The Matador was transferred to East Yorkshire Motor Services, Hull, where it served into the late 1980s.

South Wales 345, t/p 582 WP (300 CUH)

Leyland Tiger Cub 345 was converted to a towing vehicle for Haverfordwest in April 1978. Still carrying its original number, it was numbered 65 in the service fleet. South Wales renumbered some of its service fleet in October 1981, but not all new numbers were applied. 65 was withdrawn in December 1982

South Wales 14/5 (13 CNY), Neath Garage

Leyland Tiger Cub 316 (13 CNY) was converted to a trainer in June 1974, numbered 14 (later 5). A very basic conversion, simply plating over the destination box, it was withdrawn in September 1975.

South Wales 68 (WCY 701), Ravenhill Garage, Swansea

When the workshops of United Welsh at Neath were closed, South Wales provided staff transport, using two of the famous single-deck half-cab AEC Regents to transport staff to its own workshop at Ravenhill. In May 1977 it converted two ex-United Welsh Bristol MWs: 9 (WCY 701) and 10 (WCY 704). 10 was withdrawn before 1980. 9 (WCY 701), former bus 380, was later renumbered 68, and was withdrawn later in July 1982. These vehicles probably also found use between South Wales' four locations in the city.

South Wales 53 (NOB 415M), Quadrant Bus Station, Swansea

In August 1982 South Wales purchased seven Bristol VRT with MCW bodywork from West Midlands PTE. Two (NOB 415/6M) were not used in passenger service; instead SWT converted them to driver training vehicles. They were numbered 52/3 (renumbered in March 1983 to 58/9).

Midland General t/p 185 RA, Langley Mill Garage

Though Midland General became part of Trent during the early years of the NBC, it continued to use the Midland General fleet name on vehicles for a time. Midland General's AEC Matador carried bodywork almost identical to Mansfield Districts Matador, the key difference being only the MGOC version carried a crane. Allocated to Langley Mill garage, it was replaced by Trent AEC Mandator A18 in April 1978. (P. Henson, Transport Library)

Trent T1 (LCH 326K), Derby Garage

Leyland Leopard T1 carries the standard livery for Trent trainers. This was also the livery directed by the NBC for all service vehicles. Converted in February 1981 from bus 326, it was initially numbered A59.

Trent A56 (LRC 454), Derby Bus Station

Driver trainer A56 was a Leyland PD3 (ex-bus 588) was converted in 1974. A number of this type lasted in passenger service with Trent long enough to receive NBC poppy red livery.

Trent A61 (RCH 525F), Derby Bus Station

Daimler Fleetline A61 (ex-bus 925) was converted to driver training duties in January 1981. Trent always used this plain white livery for it training fleet during its NBC years, though it usually had the addition of 'NATIONAL' corporate lettering.

Trent A15 (OCH 558L), Uttoxeter Bus Station

Trent replaced its former Bristol LD tree lopper E1 (later A28) with this Daimler Fleetline (ex-558) in August 1980, numbered A15 (later A27).

Trent A24 (JRA 331N), Derby Bus Station, 9 July 1975

Trent Ford Transit open lorry A24 (JRA 331N) is seen in Derby bus station in July 1975. Trent would paint its service vehicles in white livery lettered 'NATIONAL' as directed by the National Bus Company, though at this time it was painting its commercial vehicles in NBC poppy red livery, oddly without the fleet name – just a 'Double N' logo.

Trent CCH 921H, Derby Bus Station, 9 July 1975

Trent CCH 921H was a Bedford CF van, and though the company owned at least two Bedford CF vans, Ford Transit and Escorts were the vehicles of choice for the fleet. The van is seen in poppy red livery outside the bus station in Derby in July 1975.

United 69, t/p 014 HN, Newcastle City Centre

As replacement for its AEC Matadors, United Automobile took two Ford D towing conversions built by United Counties in 1977. Numbered 68 (t/p 017 HN) for Bishop Auckland/Darlington and 69 (t/p 014HN), 69 had served with United Counties (1029) briefly before being transferred north. The company also operated two similar Ford D recoveries, 70/71, which were rebuilt in the company's own workshop. 71 was allocated to Middlesbrough, while 70 was possibly used from Central Workshops in Darlington. They were painted in yellow livery, though some were later painted poppy red. (G. Bubb)

United 61, t/p 017HN, Vernon Road, Scarborough, February 1977

Seen across the road from United's Scarborough garage is the company's well-known Bristol K5G towing conversion 61, which was converted in 1956 from BD023, an ECW double-deck. Originally numbered ED023, in 1968 it became 35, then finally 61 in 1971. It was allocated to Scarborough from 1975 until its withdrawal in 1978. It was saved for preservation in pre-NBC livery in the North East.

United 81 (821 YEH)

Leyland Leopard L2/Plaxton Panorama coach 1168 had an interesting history. New to Michelin as a demonstrator for it rubber tires in 1963, it passed to Ribble (1060) soon after. In 1976 it was transferred to United Automobile, where it carried all over NBC coach white. United painted it in poppy red bus livery and used it to transport staff to its Central Works. It became a towing vehicle in 1977, receiving the number 81 in the service fleet for use at Durham garage. It was withdrawn in the mid-1980s. (G. Bubb)

United 1071, t/p 015 HN, Newcastle Gallowgate Garage, October 1982

Though United operated Ford D recovery lorries, they were not entirely successful. For its next generation of towing vehicles it used former coaches. Former Leyland Leopard coach 1071 (originally with Midland Red) was converted in August 1982. Painted in all-over poppy red, it carried its PSV number until renumbered 82 in July 1983.

United 82, t/p 015 HN, Newcastle Gallowgate Garage

United later cut back 82 behind the rear axle to improve its performance in its new role. It would pass to newly formed bus company 'Northumbria' with the privatisation of United Automobile in 1986.

United 104 (JNU 987D) and 105 (JUN 988D), Redcar Garage

In the late 1970s United had a fleet of ten Bristol FLFs for its training vehicles, seven ex-Trent and three from Southdown. Two of the Trent batch, 104/5, acquired in 1978, are seen at their home garage of Redcar. United painted its trainers in an attractive cream livery with a red band, a reversed version of its former Tillings livery. United operated a large training fleet, moving from Bristol LD to FS and finally FLFs. A few Bristol MWs were also used as trainers in the same livery.

United 106 (JNU 989D) and Northern T321 (BUF 254C), Stockton, June 1985

An interesting photograph showing two companies training vehicles together, United Automobile Bristol FLF 106 of Middlesbrough garage and Northern General T321 (DT32), a former Southdown Leyland PD3/4 that became a Northern trainer in October 1977. This illustrates the freedom each fleet had in livery application when it was not a PSV.

United 100 (JNU 983D), Darlington Garage

Two driver trainers, 100 and 110, depart from United's Darlington garage in the early 1980s. Trainers 100–107 were formerly with Trent in 1978 and 108–110 were from Southdown in 1977.

United Counties 1004 (KBD 713D)

United Counties 1004, a Bristol FS6G, was a tuition vehicle and tree lopper converted in 1981 from bus 713. The front of the upper deck could be removed as required for tree cutting. It towed a trailer for the cuttings, which is just visible behind the vehicle. This vehicle passed to Milton Keynes City Bus in January 1986, lasting until June 1988. Note Oxford South Midland's planning bus 339 (339 TJO), illustrated earlier, repainted for exhibition use, on the left.

United Counties 1005 (KBD 714D), Northampton Central Works

United Counties next conversion was another Bristol FS (714) in January 1981, 1005, but solely as a tuition vehicle. Seen possibly newly converted outside the company's Central Workshops in Northampton, 1005 would eventually pass to Fife Scottish Omnibus in the 1990s.

United Counties 1044 (PBD 461V), Northampton Garage, 2 August 1985

United Counties commercial fleet during NBC days was made up of Morris Marina and Vauxhall Chevanne vans – Bedford CF vans and pick-ups and Bedford KDL/TL for its large lorries. Bedford CF van 1044 (PBD 461V) stands outside Northampton garage in the mid-1980s. In September 1985 it was transferred into the United Counties engineering fleet, which adopted a light blue and white livery.

United Counties 50 (XBM 216K), Northampton Central Works

A fascinating photograph showing the United Counties Ford D towing conversions in progress. Two unidentified tractor units stand with the Austin Morris JU250 pick-up 50 (XBM 216K), which was new in July 1972 for use at Bedford garage, but had been transferred to the Central Works building department before withdrawal in March 1978. (J. Harrington)

United Counties Northampton Central Works, June 1976

Three driver tuition vehicles, 1026 (523 JRA/ex-bus 574), 1024 (WAL 437/ex-bus 575) and 1025 (623 LFM/ex-bus 579), are seen in United Counties Central Workshops when newly converted in 1976. All three of these Bristol LDs were secondhand from Midland General (485), West Riding (416) and Crosville (DLG 613) respectively. At this time the company only painted the front and rear in yellow, retaining the NBC green on the rest of the vehicle. Also just visible are two of the Ford D towing conversions and a Morris Marina van.

Western National RV8, t/p 754 FX Weymouth Bus Rally

Weymouth Garage's AEC Matador RV8 (PFJ 850M) is seen at a local display in the mid-1970s. RV8 was purchased as late as May 1970. Western National owned seven AEC Matadors. Two retained their original cabs, while the other five were rebuilt by the company. RV5/6 were rebuilt to the same design as RV8, seen here. Apart from temporary use, the Western National group did not favour converted buses for towing in the NBC era.

Western National RV4, t/p 671 Y, Taunton Garage

Matador RV4 displays the earlier style of bodywork that was also used on RV3. RV4 (873 DUO), purchased in December 1958, was the company's first Matador, though it is not known if it operated with the company before rebuilding with its new bodywork. Note the small name 'Bimbo' painted above the windscreen. (G. Bubb)

Royal Blue RV9 (RXP 587), t/p 264 EL, Bournemouth Royal Blue Garage

Western National also owned two ex-AFS 'Green Goddess' Bedford RLs. RV9 carried Royal Blue fleet names. Purchased in April 1972, it was allocated to the company's Royal Blue Rutland Road garage in Bournemouth. Western National's other similar conversion was RV10 (NYR 440), which was bought in 1974 and allocated to St Austell garage.

Devon General RVₙ (MAE 142F), t/p 197 TT, Exeter Garage

In December 1974, Western National purchased this ex-BRS AEC Mandator and converted it to a towing vehicle for use from its Central Workshops in Laira, Plymouth. It moved to Exeter garage in July 1975, where it remained in use with Devon General after it was privatised. Western National also operated a very similar conversion: RV2 (UPP 608E), a Leyland Octopus that differed in details around the cabin roof.

Western National TVₙ (YDL 316), Exeter Bus Station

Western National TV1 carrying Cornish Busways fleet names was a former Southern Vectis Bristol FS6G (571). Transferred in 1980, Western National initially converted this to a driver training vehicle but later modified it again in November 1983 to allow for tree cutting.

Western National TU3 (MOD 956), Bristol, October 1980

Mobile training unit TU3, a Bristol LS5G, was new to Western National in July 1953 as 1665. It had carried both Western and Southern National fleet names before being converted to this role in November 1970 for use from Taunton. In this guise it carried joint WNOC, SNOC and Greenslade's fleet names. In May 1971 it became a driver/conductor trainer, and then from 1978 it was used as a MAP survey office, lettered 'Bus Passenger Survey'. From March 1980 it was on loan to Bristol Omnibus, for passenger survey work at Marlborough Street bus station in Bristol. After return to Western National it was sold in January 1981.

Red Bus 9424 (A331 ATT), Barnstable Garage, 1984

North Devon Limited, later trading as Red Bus, was formed in 1983 covering service previously operated by Western National in North Devon. It numbered its service fleet in the 9xxx series. 9424 was a LDV Freight Rover 350D light lorry.

Yorkshire Woollen A3, t/p 113 HD, Mirfield, July 1975

AEC Matador A3 was converted by Yorkshire Woollen District and allocated to its Savile Town garage in Dewsbury. Under the NBC Yorkshire Woollen and West Riding operated jointly, the service fleet was numbered into a common series in 1975. In the early 1970s, the joint fleet operated two Matadors, A1 and A3, and two Bedford RLs, A2 and E5.

Yorkshire Woollen E5, t/p 127 HD, Savile Town Garage, Dewsbury

West Riding and Yorkshire Woollen operated two Bedford RLs both as towing only vehicles. They were near identical conversions using Harrington bus panels. E5, seen above, was converted in February 1970 but was out of use by 1976 and stood in the yard of Savile Town garage in Dewsbury for a number of years. The other Bedford RL, A2 (shown in the first volume), lasted longer. Identification between the two was by minor details such as the trim line around the windscreen, though only A2 carried a NBC fleet name.

West Riding/Yorkshire Woollen A15 (KHL 845)

West Riding and Yorkshire Woollen used this attractive cream livery with a black stripe for its joint trainer fleet. A15 was a Guy Arab IV converted in July 1975. Note a rare glimpse of Morris Marina service van A10 on the left.

West Riding/Yorkshire Woollen A23 (LHL 159F)

West Riding/Yorkshire Woollen converted a number of Leyland Panthers/Roe to driver trainers. A23 was converted in May 1980. West Riding/Yorkshire Woollen had a fleet that contained a number of untypical body types for the NBC, such as Roe, as the fleet had been independent until 1969.

West Riding/Yorkshire Woollen A17 (HHL 738L), Wakefield Bus Station

West Riding/Yorkshire Woollen reused its A prefix service fleet numbers. The latest A17 driver trainer was a Bristol VRT (ex-bus 738). Previously A17 was a Guy Arab IV and a Bristol RELH. Interestingly when this photograph taken in the mid-1980s the companies were using a livery similar to that used by Yorkshire Traction for its training vehicles.

West Riding/Yorkshire Woollen A11 (UHD 912R), Dewsbury Head Office

A rare photo of a West Riding/Yorkshire Woollen service van. Ford Transit A11 (UHD 912R) was new in 1977. Details of the companies' service fleet is scarce.

West Riding/Yorkshire Woollen PHL 433M, Coliseum Coach Station, Blackpool, 3 July 1975

West Riding/Yorkshire Woollen Ford A0509 open lorry (reported as A17) is seen with a load of coach seats at Blackpool's Coliseum coach station, a location guaranteed to be full of NBC coaches in 1970s summers, but a non-Ribble NBC service vehicle makes an unusual sight. Possibly picking up seats from the local Duple factory, the drivers make use of NBC facilities. (M. Street)

West Yorkshire 4032, t/p 602 WT, York Garage

West Yorkshire converted two Bristol L5G and a longer Bristol LWL with similar coach-built bodywork. 4032 was converted from bus YSG103 (FWX 830) in 1964 to towing vehicle Y1032 for York garage. The service fleet was renumbered from a 10xx series to 40xx in 1970. In NBC service 4032 carried the fleet name York – West Yorkshire in the style directed by the City Council for York allocated vehicles on its joint services.

West Yorkshire 4022, t/p 598 WT, and 4042 (NWT 689K)

While working a National Express duty, United 6036 (OHN 720J), a dual-purpose Bristol RE, receives assistance from neighbouring West Yorkshire in the form of 4022 and 4042. 4022 was purchased by the company in 1958, an AEC Matador, formerly an RAF vehicle (22AN58) that the company rebuilt with a coach-built body with newer style AEC grill and Harvey Frost crane. Also present is West Yorkshire Ford Escort Mk 1 van 4042 (NWT 698K).

West Yorkshire 4025 (BWY 991), Harrogate Garage

New as long ago as 1937, Bristol K5G 359 was rebodied in 1949 and renumbered to DG13 in 1954. It was converted by the company in 1960 to a tree lopper (1025) and renumbered in 1971 to 4025. Seen here at the rear of Harrogate's Grove Park garage in the 1970s, it would occasionally be used as a towing vehicle when a garage's vehicle was under repair. Amazingly it lasted until June 1980, when it was sold into preservation.

West Yorkshire 4046 (WWX 442L), Keighley, August 1975

New in 1973, Ford Transit depot van 4046 was photographed in Keighley in August 1975. Not obvious in this photograph but 4046 (WWX 442L) was in a dark green livery, which West Yorkshire, a poppy red bus fleet, used for its service fleet until the 1980s.

Yorkshire Traction RV2, t/p 487 HE, Wombwell Garage

To supplement the Matador at Barnsley and replace the cutdown Tiger Cub at Rawmarsh, Yorkshire Traction purchased two Leyland Lynx former tipper lorries in 1977. L2 (later RV2), seen above, was fitted with a Holmes twin boom recovery crane, while the other L5 (later RV3) had a simple single bar fitment. L5 was confusingly also fitted with a Buffalo cab. The company would change to white, then poppy red liveries for these vehicles. (J. Harrington)

Yorkshire Traction L10 (VHE 201)

When the NBC corporate image was introduced, Yorkshire Traction used this yellow and black warning stripe addition to the bus livery for training vehicles, as seen on ex-bus 706, a Northern Counties-bodied Leyland PD3 trainer in 1974. L10 was converted in May 1974 and lasted until May 1979.

Yorkshire Traction L15 (CHE 295C), Barnsley Bus Station

Yorkshire Traction's next livery for training vehicles was cream with a red band, as seen on Leyland Leopard L15, former bus 328. It was converted in June 1977, only seeing two years in training use, being withdrawn in September 1979.

Yorkshire Traction T4 (JHE 520E)

The company's final version of training livery is seen on T4, a 1967 Leyland Leopard with Marshall dual-purpose bodywork (ex-bus 220). Converted in April 1979, it was withdrawn in July 1984.

Yorkshire Traction T8 (MCN 832L)

The CN registration gives a clue that this Leyland National started life with Northern General, originally as bus 32L, later 4433. Yorkshire Traction converted for its new role in May 1984. The use of a Leyland National in the service fleet was unusual, though by 1984 the early versions had been in service for twelve years. Interestingly this vehicle was acquired by West Riding after privatization, who returned it to PSV use in its Sheffield & District fleet (number 92).

Yorkshire Traction PHE 184M

As with many NBC fleets, photographs of their commercial vehicles are relatively rare. This Yorkshire Traction Ford Transit van is no exception. The company had Morris Minor 1000 vans and a couple of Land Rovers at the start of the corporate era but settled on Fords for its vans until privatisation. The company has used standard 5-inch-high fleet name transfers, necessitating the two lines of text.

Samuelsons SLC 535L, Heathrow, 14 July 1973

A rare photograph of SLC 535L, which was part of the National Travel South East (Samuelsons) fleet. An Austin Morris J4 open back vehicle, it was caught at Heathrow in July 1973.

Greenslades RV1, t/p 112 FJ (HFJ 930E), Greenslades Garage, Exeter, 18 May 1975

Greenslades Ford D recovery vehicle has only the double N logo on the side to give away its ownership. New in April 1967 and rebuilt by Dawlish Coaches as their recovery lorry, Greenslades had loaned it from June 1974, then purchased it in October 1974. Later it would pass into National Travel South West, when the use of the Greenslades name was discontinued. (D. Mant)

Wessex t/p 866 HT, Wessex Garage, Kingswood, Bristol

This National Wessex Leyland Beaver recovery vehicle was new in 1969 (registered SAD 341G) as a tractor unit. Purchased secondhand, the company rebuilt it in 1977. Wessex/NTSW named its coaches and this vehicle was named 'The Duke of Wessex'. It later gained National Travel South West fleet names.

Wessex t/p 335DG (539 UHT), Wessex Garage, Kingswood, Bristol

Wessex's other recovery lorry was a Bedford KFL, which was bought secondhand in August 1974 and rebuilt with a girder jib fitted on the open long wheelbase chassis. Little is documented about National Central Activities Group service vehicles. (J. Harrington)

NT South West YHT 953, Shamrock & Rambler Garage, Bournemouth, August 1976

National Travel South West Bristol LD6B publicity unit YHT 953 was formerly Bristol Omnibus L8452 of 1957. It had been transferred to NTSW in November 1974, and initially served as a waiting room at Aust Services on the M4, an interchange point for National Travel cross-country coach services. Later it became a publicity vehicle based at NTSW garage in Kingswood, Bristol. It was sold in April 1979.

National Travel East DHD 235E, Charlotte Road Garage, Sheffield

National Travel North East used two former Leyland Leopard coaches for towing duties, a simple conversion involving a towbar fitment and the removal of most of the seats. DHD 235E was at Sheffield and DHD 236E at Liversedge garage near Heckmondwicke. At this time devoid of any lettering, Sheffield's DHD 235E was new to Yorkshire Woollen District in 1967, passing to Hebble when YWD lost its coaching fleet. Hebble later became part of NT North East. It was sold *c.* 1983.

National Travel East, t/p 281 WA

Little is known about this Scammel Routeman operated by NT North East from its Charlotte Road garage in Sheffield. Purchased secondhand in May 1979, the same time as the Foden based at its Liversedge garage, both had the unusual 'Chinese Six' axle arrangement. This vehicle would later be painted all-over yellow, with NBC logos on the cab doors. (J. Harrington)